Surviving Jail or Prison
Creative Writing to Help You Grow

The day is passing,
another day, and here I lie with no thoughts,
no activity, no growth.
Would anything change if I were dead?
Would anyone care?

I am paying attention,
listening, watching,
staying alert.
I must do that in this place,
every day, every hour.
It is dangerous here.

Could he return to the way it was, where he was, back then when life was awesome? Of course not. Never.

He arrived and knew
that all was lost.
No more freedom.
No more choices.
If only he hadn't taken
that chance.

Just under the gift
was the unexpected,
a danger,
death.
But he never saw it
until it was too late.

by C. Mahoney

Life is about choices...

As I wandered down the trail, I came upon a fallen tree blocking my path. So, I took a deep breath and _____

_____

_____

_____

_____

_____

_____

_____

_____

_____

The toad looked at the passing fly and decided that it just wasn't the right thing to do.

_____

_____

_____

_____

_____

_____

_____

_____

_____

_____

He looked at the wasp and reached out his hand, thinking that _____

_____

_____

_____

_____

_____

_____

_____

_____

_____

_____

_____

As the beetle crawled toward the sweet nectar, it sensed a darkness, an evil, just on the other side of what could be ecstasy. _____

_____

_____

_____

_____

_____

_____

_____

_____

_____

Unable to stop its downward plummet, the aging leaf wondered if this was it, if this was the end that others spoke of in the dark silence of night. _____

_____

_____

_____

_____

_____

_____

_____

_____

_____

The hover fly knew that it was impervious. It could go where it wanted, do what it wished, and no one would bother it. That is what mimicry does, pretending, faking it. It protects you from those who might know the truth and do you harm. But then a shadow crossed overhead and his thoughts moved to concern, worry, and then fear. _____

_____

_____

_____

_____

_____

_____

_____

The zebra swallowtail landed among the broken twigs and muddy leaves. What is this? What happened? How have I come to be what I am, so majestic, so transformed, so different? _____

_____

_____

_____

_____

_____

_____

_____

_____

The rat snake slithered across the trail, slowly, silently, sneaking up on the hungry mouse unaware. Soon. Very soon. And then, _____

_____

_____

_____

_____

_____

_____

_____

_____

_____

I am unbeatable. I am the best. I am awesome. No one can out race me. No one can escape my wrath. _____

_____

_____

_____

_____

_____

_____

_____

_____

_____

_____

The green tree frog waited. It was good at that, silently passing each day's hours with the hope that the night would bring something meaningful. Hoping. Dreaming. Of her.

_____

_____

_____

_____

_____

_____

_____

_____

_____

The door that provides your entrance

                    is also the means of your escape,
        so don't hear it's clatter with anger,
        don't see it's closing with frustration.
View it as a goal, a challenge,

           something that is to be.

                  Let it be the symbol

        that gives you hope,
        for a better tomorrow,
        a happier and richer freedom,
        what awaits you one day,

        soon.

He curled his arms upward, feeling the tender legs of his visitor, touching, caressing each with the hope that she might leave behind something helpful, something wanted.

_____

_____

_____

_____

_____

_____

_____

_____

_____

The millipede only thought of escape, as the brightness exposed her to danger and death. Get away! Flee! I must not be taken alive. _____

_____

_____

_____

_____

_____

_____

_____

_____

_____

The yellow-bellied slider enjoyed basking in the sun's warmth. He liked the silent comfort that this log provided, time to daydream, time to travel among things that were not, ideas, fantasies, dreams of her. And then, with a gentle splash, she arrived. _____

_____

_____

_____

_____

_____

_____

_____

_____

Forward. Search. Wander. It is what I must do, for the others. Weariness isn't important. My own wishes are irrelevant. I must find for the others. _____

_____

_____

_____

_____

_____

_____

_____

_____

_____

_____

What have I become, once so grand and full of life, sought after, admired, worshipped? And now here I am, falling apart with each passing storm. How long must I endure this torture? How long must I weather life's passing? I am ready for the end. I want to die. Life no longer has meaning. _____

_____

_____

_____

_____

_____

_____

_____

The darkness was comfortable. It allowed me to relax, to hide my shame. I sought after it during the day, venturing out only once the sun had escaped the tree's grasp.

_____

_____

_____

_____

_____

_____

_____

_____

_____

Everyone loves me. I have no enemies. Life is what I want it to be. I am, and that is all that matters. Come see what I have become. Feel my softeness. Smell my fragrance. I am eternal. _____

_____

_____

_____

_____

_____

_____

_____

_____

Is this all there is to life, to being? Is this why I stretched and grew and worked?
Isn't there more to being alive than just this drudgery and repetition? _____

_____

_____

_____

_____

_____

_____

_____

_____

_____

_____

I watch them wander by, free to roam, free to stay, free to fly. And here I am, stuck,
miserable, angry. I am not happy. Why me? Why this torture, this isolation, this pain?
Why can't I be free? _____

_____

_____

_____

_____

_____

_____

_____

_____

_____

The wolf spider cared for her egg sac. It held those who would come afterward. The followers. The next. She did it because it was expected of her, required, programmed into her mind and legs and claws. She didn't choose to do so. It chose her. And she did not like not getting to make a choice. She did not like life's program, its expectation. And she did not like them. _____

_____

_____

_____

_____

_____

_____

Life is full of rules,

don't do this and don't do that,

stop this and stop that,

be here at this moment and there at that moment,

line up,

get your stuff,

shut up.

Well, deal with it.

Looking. Searching. Must find food. Must find someone who can fill this aching and hunger that drives me forward. Must kill. _____

_____

_____

_____

_____

_____

_____

_____

_____

_____

_____

The soldier beetle watched the clouds pass, occasionally broken up by a hawk, or a vulture, or the occasional raven. He tired of being alone. He wanted a friend, someone to talk to, someone to laugh with, someone that would let him be himself. But no one cared. No one stopped by. He was alone and he hated life. _____

_____

_____

_____

_____

_____

_____

_____

He was tired of eating, tired of chewing, tired of the blandness of leaf after leaf after leaf. He wanted something new, something soft, something sweet. _____

_____

_____

_____

_____

_____

_____

_____

_____

_____

Waiting. Watching. Waiting. Watching. This was his routine. He knew it and it knew him. Life was just like he wanted it to be. Routine. Order. Structure. And then there was a small ripple, and _____

_____

_____

_____

_____

_____

_____

_____

_____

_____

The centipedes sat in comfort. The ant wandered by silently. Both were fighters, deadly, dangerous, but they left each other alone. They looked for easier prey. That's what predators do, they choose who to attack. And it was time to choose. _____

_____

_____

_____

_____

_____

_____

_____

_____

No one can see me. I am where I need to be. Hidden, yet not. I can wait. I am patient. I will have my revenge. _____

_____

_____

_____

_____

_____

_____

_____

_____

_____

_____

He saw it pass by once, then twice, and then he knew. It was time, his time. Memories of lively moments visited him one last time, and then everything went dark. _____

Why am I here? What have I done to deserve this? How will I endure the loneliness?

_____

_____

_____

_____

_____

_____

_____

_____

_____

_____

We made it. This is our new home. We like it here. Life is good. _____

_____

_____

_____

_____

_____

_____

_____

_____

_____

_____

The patent leather beetle was not happy. It didn't appreciate being touched, grabbed, take away. Leave me alone, it thought in useless anger. _____

_____

_____

_____

_____

_____

_____

_____

_____

_____

Where was the warning when you needed it?

Was it in her look,

or the silence that you ignored?

Was it in the moment's intensity,

blinded by anger or desire or fascination?

If only we could travel back in time and change what did happen

into what we wish had happened,

or should have happened.

If only...

The flesh fly knew that it was gross, knew that it was messy, knew, but didn't care. It was hungry, and that was what mattered. Their words of derision didn't satiate his appetite. They were irrelevant. They were stupid. _____

_____

_____

_____

_____

_____

_____

_____

_____

The crane fly knew that it didn't have much time, and so it wondered, looking, hoping to find that other. _____

_____

_____

_____

_____

_____

_____

_____

_____

_____

_____

The firefly had one thing on his mind. Her. She was perfect, beautiful, fun, if only he could find her again. Just once more. But time was passing and he was still alone. ___

_____

_____

_____

_____

_____

_____

_____

_____

_____

_____

The fishing spider felt the ripple, felt the movement, and knew that someone was vulnerable. Someone had wandered too close to the water and had become ensnared, caught, and he would soon do the unthinkable. _____

_____

_____

_____

_____

_____

_____

_____

_____

The earthworm surfaced in frustration, thoughts of uncertainty and hope clashing within.
What am I? Who am I? How do I know that one is better than the other, or more
authentic? Society expected a choice, and the earthworm couldn't decide. It wanted to be
both, but others expected a decision. _____

_____

_____

_____

_____

_____

_____

_____

The colors fascinate me, beckon me to come and feast, dine, consume, so I arrive with delight and expectation, a gift of kindness that I wish I could repay. _____

_____

_____

_____

_____

_____

_____

_____

_____

_____

What if this is a trick? What if this gift is a trap, a snare, a ploy by those in power to seize me, enslave me, imprison me? _____

_____

_____

_____

_____

_____

_____

_____

_____

_____

Twisting, turning, winding his way through the forest, he pushed himself to keep going, to gain control of all that others have, to make it his. _____

_____

_____

_____

_____

_____

_____

_____

_____

_____

_____

The dandelion could feel the wind softly touching and tickling, teasing her with gentleness, causing her to envision what was to come. _____

_____

_____

_____

_____

_____

_____

_____

_____

_____

If only I could begin again, take a different path, make better choices. If only I could

_____

_____

_____

_____

_____

_____

_____

_____

_____

_____

_____

The chatter of those around you,

the expectations,

the history and repetitions and past

forces you into a box, to act in such a way, to do things.

Try to pull yourself free and make your own choices.

Decide for yourself.

Climb out of the box.

They are not really my friends. They don't really care about me. If life throws me into the abyss, will they rush to my aid? No, of course not. They're just here for the giggles, for the good times, for the laughter and excitement and momentary pleasure.

_____

_____

_____

_____

_____

_____

_____

_____

I can become something wonderful, if I choose. _____

_____

_____

_____

_____

_____

_____

_____

_____

_____

_____

_____

These thorns are a part of who I am, the me that is within as well as the me that others see and feel. Pretending otherwise is foolish. I admit the truth, now, today. I am not perfect. _____

_____

_____

_____

_____

_____

_____

_____

_____

Where should I go? Here is full of misery and stench. There is full of hope and possibility. But how do I leave behind all that I have grown accustomed to? Can I be brave and venture into the beyond? Can I take the chance and start all over? I hope so.

_____

_____

_____

_____

_____

_____

_____

_____

Bored. I hate having nothing to do all day, just filling up my time with meaningless stuff, this, that, pretending. I want something else, something that is more than this, something real. _____

_____

_____

_____

_____

_____

_____

_____

_____

Up I go, one step at a time. I can't get there by flying. I must walk. I must feel the roughness beneath my feet. I must endure the heat. I must accept the pain. I must focus only on the space that lies just within my sight. And one day, I'll be there. _____

_____

_____

_____

_____

_____

_____

_____

_____

I know that I am special, of course, but I am surrounded by others who speak loudly of their own accomplishments, what they have done, their victories and battles, their conquests and victims. I tire of the cacophony, the lies, the bravado. But where can I go to escape. I am stuck here. Marooned. Imprisoned. _____

_____

_____

_____

_____

_____

_____

_____

So barren and empty. I feel that I am nothing in my nakedness. Worthless. Hated.

_____
_____
_____
_____
_____
_____
_____
_____
_____
_____
_____

If only I could fly. If only I could get away. _____

_____

_____

_____

_____

_____

_____

_____

_____

_____

I go down when told to go down. I stand when told to stand. I turn when told to turn. I want to make my own choices, chart my own paths, wander through places where no one has gone before. I want to be my own man. _____

_____

_____

_____

_____

_____

_____

_____

_____

Are you an individual or a member of a group?

Are you a follower or a leader?

Are you compliant or someone who questions?

Are you the decision-maker or the one who doesn't think?

Are you the guy who cares or the guy who sits in silence?

Be honest with yourself!

You know the truth.

You know who you are.

The path isn't easy. So many obstacles lie in my way, but I will get there, one way or another, if only I focus on the walk, on today, on this moment. _____

_____

_____

_____

_____

_____

_____

_____

_____

I need to get out of this swamp, out of this misery, out of this place, if only for a few moments, and enjoy the pleasures of life. I want to feel the sunshine on my face and breathe the clean air of freedom. _____

_____

_____

_____

_____

_____

_____

_____

_____

I wait, because I must. _____

_____

_____

_____

_____

_____

_____

_____

_____

_____

_____

I swim because I must. I swim, like others who look like me but aren't. I swim, and wish that I could be somewhere else. I swim, with no identity, no uniqueness, just another fish. Lethargy seeks to overtake me, so I swim. _____

_____

_____

_____

_____

_____

_____

_____

_____

I have fallen, once strong and rooted and able, but now just in the way of those who walk by. What have I done? How could I have been so foolish? _____

_____

_____

_____

_____

_____

_____

_____

_____

_____

There will come a time when I am not here. Will anyone notice? _____

_____

_____

_____

_____

_____

_____

_____

_____

_____

_____

_____

I cling to the side of this tree, nervous, afraid of the shadow that approaches from the distance. _____

_____
_____
_____
_____
_____
_____
_____
_____
_____
_____

Nothing to do but close my eyes and dream. _____

_____

_____

_____

_____

_____

_____

_____

_____

_____

A tree fell, and the sound wasn't heard. _____

_____

_____

_____

_____

_____

_____

_____

_____

_____

_____

A road led forward. I saw but a few yards. I wanted to know more, where it led, what waited in the beyond, who I might encounter, whether happiness lay there or something else. But I wouldn't know unless I ventured, so I did. It's what bravery is all about.

_____

_____

_____

_____

_____

_____

_____

_____

Don't hide from the rain.

Feel it.

Endure it.

Let it bring a chill to your skin as it washes you clean.

Don't run from the storm.

Marvel at the lightning.

Listen for the thunder.

Dare the wind to try to knock you down, and keep you there.

Don't be silent when you know you should speak.

Tell the fool to shut up.

Tell the liar get real.

Show others that you call things as they are and aren't afraid to speak your mind.

Hiding beneath, my safety, away from the unknown that might bring pain and discomfort, or death. _____

_____

_____

_____

_____

_____

_____

_____

_____

_____

_____

Sometimes I feel that I am insignificant, just another creature on another leaf from another tree. Maybe not just sometimes. Maybe all the time. _____

_____

_____

_____

_____

_____

_____

_____

_____

_____

_____

_____

Where do I go now? What do I do? How do I turn the drudgery of endless moments into meaning and importance? _____

_____

_____

_____

_____

_____

_____

_____

_____

_____

Run, run, faster, move, go to that place and then to another, quickly, now, go, go, go.

_____

_____

_____

_____

_____

_____

_____

_____

_____

_____

The day is passing, another day, and here I lie with no thoughts, no activity, no growth. Would anything change if I were dead? Would anyone care? _____

_____

_____

_____

_____

_____

_____

_____

_____

_____

Does anyone know that I am here? Does anyone care? _____

_____

_____

_____

_____

_____

_____

_____

_____

_____

_____

I am not dangerous. When I attack, it is to survive. When I take, it is only so that I might keep living. I am not a monster. I am not evil. _____

_____

_____

_____

_____

_____

_____

_____

_____

I cannot hear you, yet still you talk. Your words wash over me, but they don't stay. Think about why, and consider me. Show that you care. Please. _____

_____

_____

_____

_____

_____

_____

_____

_____

_____

Is it wrong to take what I find? _____

_____
_____
_____
_____
_____
_____
_____
_____
_____
_____

I am paying attention, listening, watching, staying alert. I must do that in this place, every day, every hour. It is dangerous here. _____

_____

_____

_____

_____

_____

_____

_____

_____

_____

_____

He arrived and knew that all was lost. No more freedom. No more choices. If only he
hadn't taken that chance. _____

_____

_____

_____

_____

_____

_____

_____

_____

There is an edge, a danger, a place you cannot go if you wish to remain safe, remain free, remain yourself. _____

_____

_____

_____

_____

_____

_____

_____

_____

_____

He knew how to survive, how to blend in, how to be one of them. _____

_____

_____

_____

_____

_____

_____

_____

_____

_____

_____

His rough exterior, his pretending, his words, his looks, protected what was inside, the real person that he was. _____

_____

_____

_____

_____

_____

_____

_____

_____

_____

Could he return to the way it was, where he was, back then when life was awesome? Of course not. Never. _____

_____
_____
_____
_____
_____
_____
_____
_____
_____

What comes next? _____

_____

_____

_____

_____

_____

_____

_____

_____

_____

_____

Patience. That is the only way to endure the solitude and isolation. _____

_____

_____

_____

_____

_____

_____

_____

_____

_____

Just under the gift was the unexpected, a danger, death. But he never saw it until it was too late. _____

_____

_____

_____

_____

_____

_____

_____

_____

_____

_____

The little brown skink decided that he had had enough. He wanted to explore, to see, to feel, and he wasn't going to let fear get in his way. So, out he went, choosing a path that had not been traveled, making new footprints where none had been left before. _____

_____

_____

_____

_____

_____

_____

_____

_____

Walk or rest? Think or react? Wander or wait? The harvestman decided to _____

_____

_____

_____

_____

_____

_____

_____

_____

_____

_____

He could go or he could stay. It was his choice. So, he _____

_____

_____

_____

_____

_____

_____

_____

_____

_____

_____

Made in the USA
Coppell, TX
22 May 2021